Positive and Uplifting Poems & Quotes

PercyLee Anderson & D. Massey

P. Lee and Dee Books

Printed in the United States of America

ISBN:978-0-9826377-0-8

Dedications. I thank my Higher Power, my father John A. Anderson, and mother Delores E. Lewis. I would also like to thank my children Keion, Vera, Colleen, Percy, and Pharaoh. I would also like to thank my siblings James, Gregory, Robert, and Arlene, and all those who touch my life.

AUTHOR PercyLee Anderson.

I would like to thank my higher power who without I wouldn't have the courage to achieve another level in my life. I would also like to thank my daughter who without I wouldn't know what to do. Thanks for standing by me through it all. Most of all I would like to thank a dear friend Percy thanks for all the support and patience with me that you have given. Without your support wisdom and humor I don't know where I would be today. I will always be there for you Thanks.

Co- Author. D. Massey.

About The Authors.

I was born April of 1961 in the Bronx. I am the middle child of five siblings born to John A Anderson and Delores E Lewis. I was raised during the end of the Civil Rights Movement. I attended P.S. 62 and I.S 52 in the Bronx and graduated from Park West HS in Manhattan. I later join the Navy and did three and half years. I've been through my ups and downs eventually landing a job on movie locations doing parking PA work. Then after several years I started working for NYCTA as a cleaner from 2001 to 2006 until injuring myself on the job. Now I'm retired and writing. So sit back, relax and Read On.

Author PercyLee Anderson.

I was born in Queens N.Y. June of 1964. I am the oldest of five. I attended New York City Public Schools Elementary and High School I graduated from Jamaica High in Queens N.Y. I then gave birth to my daughter in 1983. It was hard trying to raise a child and further my education as well. I just keep on with one thought in my mine that I can do it. Later in my life I got involved with children. I first started out volunteering at local hospital that had children corners so children can wait while there siblings or parents see the doctor. Then I became an educator for children. I am now an Assistant Program Director for an After School Program run in N.Y.C Schools. I was aspire to start writing by a friend so readers as the Author said sit back, relax, and enjoy.

Co- Author D. Massey.

INTRO.

The words that are written in this book are words that I live by. I was raised on some and some from life experiences. So sit back, relax, and enjoy. You'll see yourself in this book, remember things in the past, what's going on right now and even prepares you for the future.

READ ON.

CONTENTS

1 Encouragements

2 Love

3 Togetherness

4 Growth

5 Feelings

6 Quotes

7 Statements

Chapter 1
Encouragements

Teacher

Lift me up, so I may see.
Lift me up, so I may be.
Take my hand and show
me the way.
So I may live and dance a
better way.
Teach me things, I need to know
so I can flourish, and prosper and
really grow.
Tell of far places where you've been
so one day I can be where you've been.

The Climb

At first a baby is conceived, that we will call the basement process. During months of forming and growing, it comes time. At birth the baby is on the main floor. Then he starts up the steps, learning how to walk and talk and play. He arrives on the first floor, where he is standing, but to short to see his reflection on the window, so he continues to climb. The steps, he climbs now are his morals, behaviors, respect and habits. He learns this from what he is taught and what he sees he has arrived on the second floor now he sees, his reflection and notices he's growing up. Then he continues to climb and learns of feelings, bad and good, positive and negative. He reached the third floor and in his reflection as a teenager, he sees different directions in life. The climb continues, he looks for parental guidance, but their not always there. He looks for friendship and receives peer pressure, he doesn't understand. Then up the next flight, where he learns of alcohol and drugs and problems. He's now on the fourth floor and in his reflection he sees and enjoys, he sings and dances, and then he gets a glimpse of the top of the stairs where serenity looms, but the set of steps in front of him bear, burdens, responsibility, hard work and maturity. He now looks at his reflection and must decide whether to continue the climb or to stay where he's at and eventually go back down

You Decide For You

Setting Your Course

We've set out on this journey together,

each coming from different direction.

Stumbling, falling, and getting up brushing our self off,

just to get back on our way.

We get our focus, find our directon,spot

our goals and SET OUR COURSE, then proceed

Listen

Your boss tells you to do this

Your girlfriend tell you don't do that

trucks blowing horns, cars screeching tires

strong winds blow, gentle rain against the window pane

neighbors yelling, shared stories with friends

for the answer to all questions

is out there, so LISTEN

Rising

Man with a regular job

don't stop stridden

for there might be something better.

Keep working, keep looking, but

don't stop providing

for one day something may come

Through, like the sun in the sky

for now, just keep RISING.

The Straight and Narrow

It's like walking a tight rope,

Balancing back and forth.

Looking for a sign or maybe just hope.

Seeking that, which can't be seen,

Trying hard to make a means.

Working, struggling to do our best

Not to go crazy or fool and act

Like a pest.

Keep my mind clear and myself as

Straight as an arrow

My life should be lived on the

STRAIGHT AND NARROW.

Goals

To prepare in everyway

that day is coming.

Get all the info and don't delay

that day is coming.

Get your suit or dress fresh press

that day is coming.

Stepping high and ready to impress

that day is coming

The interview is set and your name is called

that day is coming

Now you have the job, standing ten feet tall

that day has arrived.

Getting Things Done

Fantasies run through your mind but,

responsibility return you right on time.

Going on to do what you have too.

The time lurks, tick, tock, tick.

No shortcuts, No escapes, No fancy tricks.

Don't waste energy complaining, just get finish

before you realize it, the time has diminished.

Tired, exhausted and worn-out, now you're done.

Time to relax, guilt free, get fresh and have some fun.

WORK, CLASSWORK, HOMEWORK,

    WHATEVER

GET IT DONE

Stand Your Ground

You wonder why you feel some way.
The people around you just keep getting in
your way. They smile in your face and talk
about you behind your back. Just to
realize that their the one who's whack.
With so many emotions that your heart felt.
some even made it melt. You knew that
rumors would linger around, but you made
the choice to stand your ground.
Never let no one or nothing stop you from
your vision. Because the choice you make is
your Decision.

Chapter 2
Love

Meeting Another

Two people see each other every once in awhile.

From time to time greeting are exchanged, then time

continues. Small talk develops; each time a little more

is said. The two people are at ease with each other

talking, laughing, and being open. Speaking what's on
   their

minds, once becoming comfortable, sharing ideas,
   thoughts

and feelings, in this time emotions flare.............

The two of you make it what you want it to
   be.............

IT TAKES WORK.

Negative Emotions

Anger, Envy, Greed, and Jealousy are just a few.

These are emotions we can do with out.

They've wrecked homes and damaged more
friendships,

than car accidents. When they come upon you,
you've got

to recognize it, feel it, then turn them away.

You'll save yourself a lot of heartache and maybe even
a friend.

Life wouldn't have no balance with the good without
the bad, it's

just how you handle it. Talking is you're best means to
get anything

across. So if you feel one of these come upon you,
Stop, take a walk,

come back and have a Talk.

It just might help.

Stop

Love is a four lettered word too.

Not to be thrown around so freely.

It can fill hearts and manipulate minds

it's very dangerous in the wrong hands

but good for the spirit when used with care

so be cautious, then

PROCEED

Warm Hugs

You set my heart ablaze.

You're the center of my life in many ways

Companion to my dreams and is the main ingredient

in all my thoughts it seems.

You support me through my challenges I face and
    showed

me that healing power can be as simple as a warm and
    fond embrace.

Weekends

Its always fun and good talks

WEEKENDS

We sometime take short walks

WEEKENDS

We have laughs and intimate times

WEEKENDS

I'm never broke because you're my dime

WEEKENDS

Although we're just friends

WEEKENDS

It seems you'll always be there to the end

SEE YOU NEXT WEEKEND

My Love

It started off so simple just having something to do.
   Friendship

Turn to lovers that was beautiful for me and you.
   Sleepless nights
of love making conversation to, made us both wonder
   on what we're
going to do.

You made me feel like the warmth of the sun, the
   cuddle of a mother

Hug so safe and secure. I knew right then I never felt
   like this before.

Now wanting more than friendship trying to become
   a part of you, I
know exactly what I want to do. I'm going to love
   you till both our
lives are through. I'll walk beside you, behind and in
   front of you because
you are my boo. Cripple, blind, disable I'll be there for
   you.

Not Alone

So many people come and go.

I'm not alone.

With all the hustle and bustle of a busy day.

I'm not alone.

When the one closet to my heart is not around.

I'm not alone.

When I come home and close the door.

I'm not alone.

The one, I'm with me, myself, and I.

I'm not alone.

Chapter 3
Togetherness

Friends

Some friends are there no matter what.

Some friends are there just for the moment.

Some friends are there not at all, but some friends
are there for the long haul.

These are friends that share your thoughts and well
being
are friends you keep close to your heart.

Like the Mona Lisa, real friendship is a work of Art.

Sharing

Sharing is the act of giving to one another

not one giving, and one receiving.

Sharing thoughts and dreams, and ideas

building up stairs, and knocking down old walls

TO BUILD A BETTER TOMORROW FOR ALL.

Love For All

Love is the act of caring and sharing
Walking together, Talking together
spending time, intimately, and
with family.
Love spins like the world
love also has its ups and downs,
but through it all love will stand
the test of time.

Spending Time Together

Where are we going, I know where I been, you're my
  dear, close,

and special friend

You tell me your stories and I tell you mine and yes
  we pass a few

hours of time. Some serious, some comics, some even
  of our past

allowing our memories not to be our last.

We fashion our future, polish up the past so we store it
  all in a see

through glass.

So when the conversation ends made through out the
  night it so lovely

when we end with an embrace so tight.

A Shoudler To Lean On

He's there to comfort me when times are bad

He's there to guide me when I can't see my path

He's there to listen to all my wrath

He's there to help with all my task

He's always there being strong to guide me

through my rights and wrongs, my ups and downs

that's why I know he'll always be around

Chapter 4
Growth

Steps In Life

As we grow, its like walking up a stairwell.

Each year reaching a higher level in our youth until
maturity.

Learning manner, respect, and honor.

In maturity we sometimes forget some of the things
and is lead astray.

We must once again, get on the right landing

take a look in the mirror, for each landing has one, pull
ourselves together,

and go lean over the handrail and look up and see,

where we want to be and continue to climb.

Stopping off to look in the mirror to see if we like
what we see.

Then we continue climbing the STEPS IN LIFE.

The Dream Making It Reality

A man thinks while he's sleeping,
putting ideas and thoughts together.
He awakens to find it was all
just a dream. His mind curious
to remember the thoughts and
ideas, trying hard to piece the
entire dream together. While
awaken, he hears people talking
positive, songs with rhythm and
rhyme, a message in the wind,
he pieces what he has and goes
on living, picking up suggestions
and advice on the way, hoping
one day to return to the Dream
and make it Reality.

Eternal Life

Life is a phase to be born, to live and to die.
Birth is the first of two people joining together
to make one. Within that one, both are born
again, learning and growing to be an individual.
The individual lives for self, making mistakes, and
mishaps, but through it all, the individual pulls himself
together and gets on with life. The two people have taught
and raised up the individual, now they are tired and is put
to rest. The individual goes on with life and the two live
within, the heart and mind of the individual, Eternally.

My Father

When I was a little boy playing in the sand, I
would watch my father and wished I was a man.
I love my father and I know he loves me even though
I didn't become what he wanted me to be.
For he lived his life and I'm living mine, I'm living for
today, leaving the past behind, however, I think about
my father some of the time, my father has passed, still
he is not dead, so I have go to think about my life ahead.

Common Courtesy Is...........

A hardy greeting and a pleasant farewell,

letting another know what's going on.

Sharing plans, thoughts and ideas.

Giving a complement, when do, but

the biggest is RESPECTING a person,

their time, their space, and their feelings

when they respect you.

Give

Give a hand when you can.

Give a dime, it'll be right on time.

Give a thought, it'll be like something you bought.

Give a hearty greeting, it'll be a lovely way of meeting.

Give of your heart and you can feel apart of.

Give a high five and keep your stride.

Give of yourself.

Never

Never bite your tongue when there's something you

must say.

Never tell a friend, you'll call them back when you

weren't

anyway, you'll avoid arguments and stay friends, day

after day.

Never make a promise that you really can't do. Do

what you

can happily through and through. Never, ever tell a

person, you

love them when its not in heart. Tell the person what

you feel,

Stay there, walk away or be apart of.

Parenting

We teach the children how to walk.

Then they grow.

We teach the children how to talk.

Then they grow.

We teach them of moral and responsibility.

Then they grow.

We teach them how to act and how to be.

Then they grow

We tell them to go to school an learn.

Then they grow.

We tell them to go to work so they can earn.

Then they grow.

The children have families of their own.

Now their grown.

Life's Ride

Never be afraid to be the person you were meant to be.
Get ready for struggle, get set for heartache, go handle
your responsibility. Go far away and see places you've
never seen. After you've been through all the mess as a
teen, growing up can be beautiful, fulfilling and fun.
Some will never know the things that life has to offer
under the sun. so jump on, take a swirl, the name of this
ride is called the WORLD.

Chapter 5
Feelings

Alone

Spending quiet nights – Alone

Taking long walks – Alone

Getting to know one self

Is the hardest task of all.

Waking up – Alone

Sleeping –Alone

Thinking we need someone there,

When we haven't figure out whom

we are.

But until then we're Alone.

Find out who you are !

The Great "I Am"

There's no big Is' and little Us'

just real men and women

living from day to day.

Doing their best

and that is all that is asked.

FOR IN EACH ONE OF US THERE IS GREATNESS

A Change Of Attitude

I've had negative feelings

I have positive thoughts

I've had bad days
Today I think of positive ways.

Chapter 6
Quotes

Step By Step

Do not lead, for I may not follow

Do not follow, for I may not lead

Let's walk side by side and show

Each other the way step by step.

I CAN DO GOOD BY MYSELF

I CAN DO BETTER WITH SOMEONE

GOING IN THE SAME DIRECTION

Great minds discuss ideas

Average minds discuss events

Small minds discuss people

Put yourself above no man or woman

for everyone is created equal

if you do, you find yourself below them

EMOTIONALLY, MORALLY, SPIRITUALLY

When the pain out weighs the pleasure

you've got to go through it

to grow through it.

Plan your work and

Work that plan.

Chapter 7
Statements

Working On Ones' Self

We sit and think of things, we need to do to get our
    self together.
We eat healthy, exercise, jog and weight lift.
We shower, shave and groom, we suit up, we dress
    down, thinking
We have it all together but, the most important
of all is that we pray.

Truth

Telling a story, when you don't understand the facts,
    speaking on something,
when you don't know the truth. Leading him or her
    to believe that you
want them. Explaining directions when you don't
    know yourself, it's always
best to tell the truth, say what's on your mind and get
    your facts straight.

CPSIA information can be obtained at www.ICGtesting.com
Printed in the USA
LVOW01s2349200314

378339LV00013B/143/P